WILSON

Checked for technical accuracy by Dr. Julian C. Aldrich, Professor of Social Studies at New York University; member of the Board of Directors of the American Pioneer Trails Association.

PARENTS' MAGAZINE PRESS
52 Vanderbilt Ave., New York 17, N. Y.

THE GOLDEN SPIKE

The Story of America's
First Transcontinental Railroad

by Harold Littledale
illustrated by Tony Kokinos

The telegraph key in Western Union offices all over the country clicked suddenly to life.

The message came in a volley of dots and dashes. *To everybody: Keep quiet. When the last spike is driven at Promontory, we will say "Done."*

At the War Department telegraph office in Washington, President Ulysses S. Grant's Secretary of War, John A. Rawlins, and Civil War veteran, General William Tecumseh Sherman, stood with other government officials and military men waiting impatiently for the message to be continued.

D   Y   N   O   W

Almost ready. Hats off: prayer being offered, ticked the telegraph.

In San Francisco, Mayor A. S. Brown was writing a special greeting to be wired soon clear across the country to the mayor of New York City. In New York, Mayor A. Oakey Hall had ordered flags unfurled. Now he waited to give the word for a 100-gun salute in downtown City Hall Park.

We have got done praying, the spike is about to be presented.

People in Chicago were already forming a triumphant procession in the center of the city. By nightfall the parade would be a seven-mile chain of yelling, cheering men, women, and children.

All ready now; the spike will soon be driven. The signal will be three dots for the commencement of the blows.

In Buffalo, a crowd of businessmen shifted their feet impatiently in the city's Board of Trade rooms where the news would be rung out on a huge gong fastened to the wall. A bell clanging in the steeple of historic Independence Hall would give the word to the people of Philadelphia.

The telegraph key clicked again.

Dot!—Dot!—Dot! ("The commencement of the blows.")

A locomotive engineer in Scranton reached for the whistle rope above his head, waiting. A church deacon in

Omaha grasped the bell rope hanging from his church's steeple, waiting. Hundreds of thousands of Americans paused in what they were doing and waited with them.

Done!

A triumphant shout went up in small towns and large cities all over the country. People poured out into the streets shouting and shaking hands. Bells rang. Cannons boomed. Flags were run up. Special church services began.

Another message flashed over the telegraph wires to President Grant and the newspapers of the Associated Press.

The last rail is laid! The last spike is driven! The Pacific Railroad is completed!

At Promontory, Utah, a brand new little town about seventy miles northwest of Salt Lake City, a solid gold spike had nailed down the last rail in our country's first transcontinental railroad line.

"The long looked-for moment has arrived," wrote a *New York Times* reporter from the spot. "The inhabitants of the Atlantic seaboard and the dwellers on the Pacific slopes are henceforth emphatically one people."

It was 2:47 P.M. The date was May 10, 1869.

Today jet planes fly regularly between New York City and Seattle in a few hours. News events are flashed simultaneously on television sets from Los Angeles to Portland, Maine. It's hard to believe that Americans east and west were ever anything but "emphatically one people." But one hundred years ago—when the first transcontinental railroad was being built—our country was a very different place.

Ninety-two out of every one hundred Americans lived in the East in the 1860's. The West was 1.8 million square miles of Indian hunting grounds, rough and ready frontier towns, isolated army forts, and lonely

mining camps. Getting west was a dangerous four- to six-month journey by covered wagon across desolate prairie lands, towering mountains, and scorching deserts.

But opportunities were opening up fast all over the West. And to many Americans these opportunities were more important than the dangers.

A brave man could make his fortune out west. There was gold in California and silver in Nevada; there were fur-trading riches in Oregon country. And there was land—millions of acres of government-owned land acquired over the years by treaty, purchase, and war. Anyone willing to settle and work it could have it for practically nothing.

No wonder a popular slogan of the times was, "Go West, young man, and grow up with the country!" No wonder the talk for years had been of railways to make the long trip west faster and less difficult.

OF RAILS AND "LOCOMOTIVATORS"

Railways had been known in the United States since 1795. But they were nothing like the miles of gleaming steel tracks, the modern freight and passenger cars, and the streamlined steam, electric,and diesel locomotives we know today.

In early America a railway was simply a dirt road over which ran crude tracks of wood or stone or cast iron. There were no passenger cars. Freight cars were any wagons which could be lifted up onto the rails. "Locomotives" were teams of horses and mules.

A road of rails like this was what a Virginian named Robert Mills had in mind when he asked the U.S. Congress to back a transcontinental railroad in 1819. But the idea seemed too crude. It wasn't until twenty years later, when the first steam-powered locomotives arrived in this country from England, that there was any real excitement about the idea.

The "locomotivators," as people called the huffing, rickety steam engines on wheels of those days, were a great success. They could pull a wagon loaded with twenty-three passengers at speeds up to eighteen miles an hour. The wood needed to fire up their big steam boilers was cheap and easy to find. With their newly designed iron tracks and special freight and passenger cars, they seemed the perfect answer to the demand for a faster, more comfortable way west. Still, people doubted.

In the U.S. Senate, a famous orator and statesman, Daniel Webster, talked against the transcontinental idea. He couldn't see why anyone would *want* to go west. And he described the land beyond the Missouri River as "that vast and worthless area—that region of savages and wild beasts, of deserts, of shifting sands and whirling winds, of dust, of cactus, of prairie dogs."

But more and more people were going west anyway, and the railroads were going that way too. Small railroad lines started up in Pennsylvania, in South Carolina, in Maryland, in New York. Track laying went on at a furious pace. There were less than forty miles of railroad in the United States of 1830. Ten years later there were almost nine thousand miles.

By 1843 there were rail connections between the Atlantic coast and the Great Lakes. By 1849 railroads had gone as far as the Mississippi River and were still being built westward. The handwriting was on the wall. In 1853 Congress asked for a government survey to find the best railroad route west, from the Missouri River clear across the continent to the Pacific coast.

And in California, a year later, a brilliant young railroad construction engineer decided that, if there was to be a transcontinental railroad after all, he was going to build it. His name was Theodore Dehone Judah.

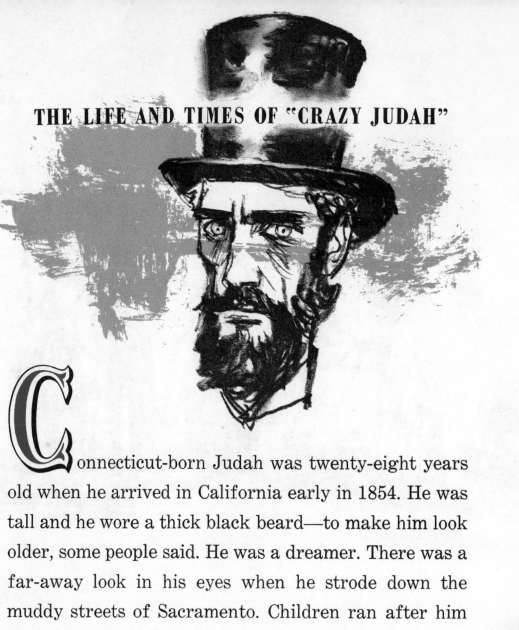

THE LIFE AND TIMES OF "CRAZY JUDAH"

Connecticut-born Judah was twenty-eight years old when he arrived in California early in 1854. He was tall and he wore a thick black beard—to make him look older, some people said. He was a dreamer. There was a far-away look in his eyes when he strode down the muddy streets of Sacramento. Children ran after him shouting, "Crazy Judah! Cra-ee-zy Judah!"

The California that Judah had come to was booming. Gold had been discovered beside John Sutter's sawmill near Coloma in 1848, and prospectors had been pouring into the state ever since. Tiny San Francisco and Sacramento had grown into thriving cities almost overnight. The shopkeepers were making fortunes selling drygoods, food, and hardware to the gold hunters.

But transportation was a problem in the California of the Gold Rush days. People and goods could hardly get around on the winding footpaths and rutted wagon trails of the new state. Railroads were needed, and wider, carefully graded wagon roads. This is where Judah came into the picture.

A group of Sacramento businessmen had hired Judah to do two jobs. The first was to survey a railroad—California's first—to run twenty-one miles between Sacramento and Folsom. The second job was to map out a wagon road running east from Sacramento, up over the jagged Sierra Nevada Mountain peaks and on to Nevada where silver mines were opening up.

The first job went quickly. Only fifteen days after he arrived in Sacramento, Judah had surveyed the route. In a year a train was running regular trips to Folsom. But the more Judah worked at mapping out a route to Nevada, the more he became sure that the wagon road should be a railroad—and not just to Nevada, but beyond, all the way to the Atlantic coast.

Leland Stanford

Collis Porter Huntington

Judah asked his employers to back this plan, but they refused. Judah talked to leading California citizens —he even staged a Pacific Railroad Convention in San Francisco—but people laughed at the idea and said "Crazy Judah" was a good nickname.

Judah decided to ask the government to back his plan, so he went to Washington. He found members of the U.S. Senate and House of Representatives more and more interested in the transcontinental railroad. But now they couldn't agree on a route for the road to follow.

It's not hard to understand why. The railroad would carry settlers and new business to the states it ran through. Each congressman wanted the route to run as close to his state as possible so that his people would benefit.

Charles Crocker

Mark Hopkins

And then there was the question of slavery which would soon plunge the country into bloody civil war. Northern congressmen wanted the transcontinental railroad to follow a northerly or central route through states where slavery was not allowed. Slave-holding southerners wanted the railroad to run through the southwest. There was a lot of hot talk, but no action.

Judah was discouraged. But his luck was about to change. Four Sacramento businessmen had caught his railroad fever.

The four were Leland Stanford, a grocer, Collis Porter Huntington and Mark Hopkins, partners in a hardware and mining equipment business, and Charles Crocker, a drygoods man. They were rich and getting richer. Later they were called "The Big Four."

The Big Four listened to Judah. They looked at his maps and surveys. Finally they agreed to give him money to build his railroad over the mountains to the silver mines in Nevada, where they could sell lots of supplies and equipment to the miners. They formed a company—The Central Pacific Railroad of California. They made Judah chief engineer of the railroad.

In Washington, Judah's luck was changing too. The year was 1861. The Civil War had begun. Southern congressmen had left the Senate and the House of Representatives. The remaining congressmen agreed on a middle route for the transcontinental railroad. In the spring of 1862 Congress passed a Pacific Railroad Act.

The Act gave Judah's Central Pacific Railroad the right to build east from Sacramento. It set up a Union Pacific Railroad and Telegraph Company to start building west from the Missouri River near Omaha, Nebraska.

It set the eastern boundary of California as the meeting place of the two railroads, but allowed whichever company reached the state line first to continue until the two roads were linked.

To encourage speed, the Act provided generous grants of government-owned land, and low-cost government loans of from $16,000 to $48,000 for each mile of railroad completed. President Abraham Lincoln signed the bill on the first of July, 1862. And one of the longest, most exciting, and strangest races in history began.

THE CENTRAL PACIFIC RAILROAD

Building a railroad is a slow business at best. But the conditions under which the Central Pacific Railroad began to build early in 1863 were the worst possible.

There was plenty of good California redwood around for railroad ties. But everything else—every nail, every spike, every hammer, every pickaxe—had to be brought to California from the East, an 18,000-mile trip by sailing ship around stormy Cape Horn at the southern tip of South America. And shipping was expensive—it cost $2,000 just in freight costs to bring the first steam locomotive to California.

Worse still, there was a shortage of workers in the California of the 1860's. Many of the younger men had gone to war. The mining boom was slowing down, but the settlers had found the California farming good and were busy with their land. Only a few drifters were willing to take on the dangerous, back-breaking work Judah's railroad offered. And these worked slowly. At the end of 1863 only eighteen miles of track were laid.

The Big Four called Judah on the carpet. They blamed him for the railroad's slow pace. Thousands of dollars were at stake in government lands and loans, they said. Speed was the most important thing.

Judah was angry. He said the most important thing was to build a good railroad. The argument went back and forth. Neither Judah nor the Big Four would budge an inch. Finally, Judah quit. The Big Four bought out his share of the railroad's stock for $100,000, and once again "Crazy Judah" made the long trip back east.

The trip was his last. Judah died of yellow fever just after he arrived in New York.

THE UNION PACIFIC RAILROAD

In the East the Union Pacific Railroad and Telegraph Company was having troubles of its own. A marvelous ground-breaking ceremony had been held near Omaha in December of 1863. But two years later, when the Civil War ended, not a rail had been laid. There were a number of reasons.

For one thing, the Civil War had taken men and money from the project. For another, there had been scandals. People said the railroad's backers had put as much money into their pockets as they had spent on the railroad.

Finally, the Union Pacific needed a leader—someone able to handle the rowdy bunch of ex-soldiers, tough Irish immigrants, and free-wheeling mule-skinners who had signed on to build the road. Such a leader was General Grenville M. Dodge who became the Union Pacific's chief engineer in 1866.

Dodge was a war hero. He had been wounded twice in battle, and he had been commended by General

Ulysses S. Grant for building railroads under heavy fire. He was an honest and fearless leader. And he knew the West—before the Civil War he had surveyed in the very country through which the railroad was to run.

Dodge quickly took charge of the Union Pacific's construction. Two hundred and sixty miles of tracks were laid down during his first year as the railroad's chief engineer—more than eight times as many as had been built in the three previous years. And this was only the warm-up. Records were to come. The Union Pacific was humming at last.

Things were humming back in California, too. "Crazy Judah" was gone. But Charles Crocker, one of The Big Four, had taken over the job of ramming the Central Pacific Railroad across the California countryside and up through the solid granite Sierra Nevada Mountain peaks.

A roaring big man—250 pounds of stubborn courage and pure energy—Charlie Crocker was an ex-New York farm boy who had made good as a drygoods salesman in California. He had none of Judah's engineering know-how. But he could lead men. And at last he had found good men to lead. They were Chinese laborers— small, wiry men in odd, down-turned basket hats and sagging blue denim suits.

By 1866 Crocker had two thousand Chinese working for his Central Pacific Railroad. In the years that followed the number grew to ten thousand. People called them "Crocker's Pets."

They were demons for work, these Chinese laborers, and it was a good thing. The work ahead was going to be harder than any railroad building ever done before.

By the spring of that same year, 1866, more than forty miles of Central Pacific track had been laid to Colfax. It had been uphill work, a climb of one thousand feet. Now there was a further climb of seven thousand feet to the summit of the Sierra Nevada and a mountain peak called Cape Horn.

Slowly the Central Pacific edged up into the mountains. "Crocker's Pets" worked from baskets swinging high above the raging American River, chipping a road along the sides of towering granite cliffs. Slowly they toiled their way up past mining camps with colorful names—*Red Dog, You Bet, Dutch Flat, Little York.*

Winter came, and heavy snows. Many of the men worked in damp semi-darkness in tunnels built underneath the snow. Others took their chances outside in screaming winds where avalanches could sweep them to sudden death in the canyons below. Half the men worked simply at shovelling the tons and tons of snow that fell in the high passes. Many died—of sickness and plain exhaustion.

Hammers and pickaxes bent useless against the solid granite mountainside. Progress could be as little as eight inches a day. But the work went on, through winter and spring.

By September of 1867 the passage across the mountains was open for train travel. Crocker said the worst was over. From now on his men could lay a mile of track a day. Nevada was in sight.

INDIANS!

While "Crocker's Pets" were fighting their way through the blizzards of the high Sierra Nevadas, General Grenville M. Dodge's Union Pacific men were fighting the Indians of the Nebraska and Wyoming plains.

They had been warned. Shortly after the Union Pacific had laid its first tracks, Red Cloud, a great Sioux warrior chief, had sent the railroad men a message. "We do not want you here," he said. "You are scaring away the buffalo." But the railroad had pushed ahead, and the

Sioux and the Cheyenne Indians had gone on the war-path.

Their attempts to stop the railroad were almost funny at first. One Indian brave tied the end of a rawhide rope around his waist and lassoed the tall smokestack of a passing locomotive. He went flying off his horse as the train charged on.

Another time a band of Indians tried stopping a train by holding a rope taut across the tracks. The train smashed into the rope and the Indians went sailing.

But as the railroad pushed ahead through Nebraska and into Wyoming, the Indian raids became more serious—and more deadly.

Led by chiefs named Spotted Tail and Turkey Leg, Indians of the Sioux and Cheyenne tribes raided railroad camps where they stampeded horse and mule herds, and stole guns, food, and clothing. They tore down telegraph wires and pried up tracks. They massacred surveying parties and scalped track-laying crews.

The Indians stepped up their raids and General Dodge ordered every railroad worker to carry a gun. The crews' sleeping cars were turned into armed forts. Dodge asked for government troops from Washington and soon they came—under General William Tecumseh Sherman and a young, fire-eating cavalry colonel named George Armstrong Custer.

[Custer was to become famous ten years later when he and a party of 264 cavalrymen were massacred at the battle of the Little Big Horn in Montana territory.]

Still the Union Pacific pushed on. By the end of 1867 it had moved ahead 240 miles to Cheyenne, Wyoming. There the crew set up camp for the winter.

THE RACE TO THE GOLDEN SPIKE

With spring, the pace of the two railroads quickened. Surveyors for both roads worked far ahead of the other crews, staking out the routes east and west. Behind them, graders and bridge-building gangs made the road level and built wooden bridges across rivers and gullies. Then came the track-laying teams.

Horse or mule teams pulled open supply trucks holding ties, rails, and spikes to the end of the track. They stopped. The animals were unhitched. Quickly, ties were dropped along the roadbed. At the foreman's shouted order, "Down!" rails were laid on the ties, "gauged" to be sure they were exactly four feet, eight and a half inches apart, and spiked down while a small horse pulled the supply truck ahead. When the truck was empty it was tipped sideways off the tracks. Another truck with more ties and rails and spikes was whipped forward to take its place.

"Hurry!" was the word you heard most among the railroad crews now. "Crocker's Pets" had been making a steady mile a day ever since they had crossed the California state line and moved into Nevada. But messages from the Union Pacific said General Dodge's men had laid three miles in a single day, then four.

Crocker's men stepped up their work and put down a record seven miles in a day. The Union Pacific raised it to seven and a half.

The Union Pacific's foreman said his men could lay eight miles of track in a single day. He challenged Crocker to do as well. Crocker laughed and said his men could do ten.

The Union Pacific's vice president, Thomas C. Durant, sent Crocker a message: "Ten thousand dollars if you can do it before witnesses."

"We'll notify you," Crocker replied.

The two railroads edged closer and closer. By the spring of 1868 the Central Pacific had passed through a little wagon stop called Reno and moved into the Nevada desert lands. Crocker's men were going at a good speed now. They laid two miles, then three miles a day. But there was no hint of a try for ten.

The Union Pacific rushed ahead through Wyoming —past Laramie and into Benton. The Central Pacific snaked its way across the Nevada desert and along the Humboldt River.

By September, General Dodge's ten thousand laborers and five hundred horse and mule teams had passed through the burning Red Desert and the waterless country of the Bitter Creek Basin. By the end of 1868, they had laid another 425 miles of rails and were camped in Wasatch, Utah, sixty-five miles from Ogden.

The Central Pacific was pressing on through Wells, Nevada, toward the Utah border. The two roads were only three hundred miles apart now. But Crocker only smiled when he was asked about the ten miles of track he had said his men could lay in a day.

Helped by sturdy track-laying teams provided by Brigham Young, the Salt Lake City Mormon leader, the men of the Union Pacific and the Central Pacific worked on through the winter. By March 3, 1869, the Union Pacific had reached Ogden where it was met by a giant parade and banners reading:

Meanwhile, the Central Pacific's men pushed on and on, crossing the state border into Utah. The railroads were forty miles apart, thirty miles apart, twenty. The transcontinental railroad was almost joined. And then, on April 28, Crocker announced, "Tomorrow we'll lay those ten miles." He invited doubters to come see for themselves.

The following day "Crocker's Pets" were up at dawn. Their hammers were ringing on the rails by seven in the morning. Supply trucks hurtled back and forth between the track-laying teams and five trains loaded with supplies for the day's work. The crews were laying five pairs of rails a minute as the foreman shouted, "Down!—Down!—Down!"

Six miles of rail had been laid by one-thirty in the afternoon and still the workers sweated on. Tie after tie was dropped in place. Rail after rail was set and spiked. Froth-covered mule and horse teams galloped up and down the ever longer line of track. Crocker rushed this way and that—urging his men on, yelling, threatening.

At last, as the sun went down and the day's-end whistle blew, the workers dropped their hammers and slumped to the ground. They had laid ten miles of track, and 1,800 feet more for good measure. Crocker had won his ten-thousand-dollar bet. The tracks of the two railroads were now less than ten miles apart, and there was no possibility of the Union Pacific matching the Central's feat.

Three days later the gap between the two railroads had narrowed to a single rail's length. The Union Pacific had laid 1,086 miles of track. The Central Pacific Railroad had laid 690.

Early on the morning of May 10, 1869, a nine-year-old boy climbed up to the top of a telegraph pole in Promontory, Utah. This is what he saw:

Promontory itself was a jumble of tents and wooden shacks. The main street was a muddy pathway. Only the shining twin sets of railroad tracks, entering the town from east and west and stopping just short of a meeting, seemed permanent.

Facing each other across the gap in the rails were two steam locomotives—the Central Pacific's *Jupiter* and the Union Pacific's unnamed *Number 119*. Their steel-plated sides gleamed with polishing. Their smoke stacks sparked and billowed smoke with a full head of steam.

Promontory was jammed and noisy. Close to 1,500 sightseers milled around the hooting locomotives, shouting to make themselves heard. Four companies of infantry soldiers drilled. Two brass bands played patriotic songs and operatic airs. A telegraph operator seated at a wooden table near one of the locomotives shouted at people to move away so he could see what was going on. Newspaper reporters from all over the United States were everywhere, asking questions and taking notes.

At last the ceremonies began. The last tie—a block of polished California laurel wood—was put in place. Chinese laborers carried the last rail to the roadbed and laid it down. The Reverend John Todd of Pittsfield, Massachusetts, led a prayer.

Speeches were made. "The Star Spangled Banner" was sung. A railroad spike of solid gold was presented and set into a hole especially drilled for it. Now everything was ready. When the golden spike was driven, the two roads would become one.

Leland Stanford stepped forward to represent the Central Pacific Railroad of California. He raised the silver-headed sledge hammer which had been made especially for the occasion. He took a deep breath, swung the hammer—and missed! The crowd cheered anyway.

Now Thomas C. Durant of the Union Pacific Railroad and Telegraph Company seized the hammer. He swung—and he missed too! The crowd cheered again, and guests of the two railroads stepped up to the golden spike and drove it home. The cheers became a deafening roar as the two locomotives—the Central's *Jupiter* and the Union's *Number 119*—first one, then the other, chugged forward and back across the last rail.

• • •